THIS BOOK BELONGS TO...

Name: Age:

Favourite player:

2022/2023

My Predictions... Actual...

Forest's final position:

Forest's top scorer:

Premier League winners:

Premier League top scorer:

FA Cup winners:

EFL Cup winners:

Contributors: Peter Rogers

A TWOCAN PUBLICATION

ISBN: 978-1-914588-67-9

PICTURE CREDITS:
Action Images, Alamy, Press Association, Nottingham Forest Football Club.

CONTENTS

GOAL OF THE SEASON

Jack Colback's strike against West Bromwich Albion was voted by supporters as our 2021/22 Goal of the Season - and what a strike it was!

Looking to respond following an unfortunate 1-0 defeat to Luton Town on Good Friday, The Reds hosted West Brom on Easter Monday night looking to return to winning ways and cement their place in the play-off positions.

After making a bright start on the night, The Reds were awarded a penalty when Darnell Furlong deliberately handled James Garner's goalbound effort. Furlong was dismissed for a second yellow card, with Brennan Johnson stepping up and finding the net from 12 yards.

Ryan Yates headed in from Garner's corner to double Forest's lead just four minutes later, before Colback stole the show with a simply sensational goal to make it 3-0 in first half stoppage time.

Taking a throw-in on the left-hand side, Colback found Johnson who flicked the ball back over a defender's head, before the 32-year-old unleashed a first-time, left-footed, dipping volley over David Button and into the far corner from 25 yards.

Colback's reaction only summed up everybody's reaction to the goal, but he would later go on to insist that it was a shot and by no means a cross...

Sam Surridge wrapped up the three points in second half injury time when he coolly found the net following good work by Philip Zinckernagel to make it 4-0, sparking a run of four successive victories in the business end of the campaign.

THE RUNNERS-UP

Djed Spence's strike against QPR was a narrow second. Trailing 1-0 at the break, the wing-back levelled the scoring for The Reds in some style.

Receiving the ball 25 yards from goal, Spence unleashed a fierce, curling effort which flew into the top-right corner.

Lewis Grabban's goal against Birmingham City was voted third. The striker picked up the ball inside the Birmingham half before letting fly from 25 yards, seeing his effort nestle into the top-right corner to break the deadlock at St. Andrew's.

JESSE LINGARD

11

Defending is not just about stopping the attackers and clearing your lines. Making the best of possession you have just won is vital - although the danger has to be cleared, it is important for your team to keep hold of the ball.

SOCCER SKILLS

LONG PASSES

When passing your way out of defence, and short, side-foot passes are not possible, the longer pass, driven over the heads of midfield players, can be used.

EXERCISE

In an area 40m x 10m, A1 and A2 try to pass accurately to each other, with a defender B, in the middle between them. Player B must attempt to stop the pass if possible, and A1 and A2, must keep the ball within the area of the grids.

After each successful long pass, the end player will exchange a shorter pass with B before passing long again, thus keeping the exercise realistic and also keeping the defender in the middle involved. The player in the middle should be changed every few minutes, and a 'count' of successful passes made for each player.

KEY FACTORS

1. Approach at an angle.
2. Non-kicking foot placed next to the ball.
3. Eye on the ball.
4. Strike underneath the ball & follow through.

Practice is the key to striking a consistently accurate long pass and to developing the timing and power required.

The same end result could be achieved by bending the pass around the defender instead of over him, and this pass could be practised in the same exercise, by striking the football on its outer edge (instead of underneath) which will impart the spin required to make the ball 'bend' around the defender - not an easy skill!

PREMIER LEAGUE 2022/2023 SQUAD

1 DEAN HENDERSON

GOALKEEPER DOB: 12/03/1997

Born in Whitehaven, Henderson started his career with Carlisle United before moving to Manchester United in 2011. After signing a professional contract in 2015, Henderson had loan spells with Stockport County, Grimsby Town, Shrewsbury Town and Sheffield United before joining The Reds in the summer of 2022. Winner of the U20 World Cup in 2017, the goalkeeper made his senior England debut in November 2020 at Wembley as the Three Lions beat the Republic of Ireland.

2 GIULIAN BIANCONE

DEFENDER DOB: 31/03/2000

A former France youth international, Biancone signed for Forest from French Ligue 1 outfit Troyes in July. After making his senior debut for Monaco in a Champions League fixture against Atlético Madrid in November 2018, the defender spent two seasons on loan with Belgian side Cercle Brugge before returning to France with Troyes in 2021.

3 STEVE COOK

DEFENDER DOB: 19/04/1991

Following ten years with AFC Bournemouth, Cook joined Nottingham Forest in January 2022. Starting his career at Brighton & Hove Albion, the defender had loan spells in the lower leagues before moving to the South Coast in 2011. Cook helped Bournemouth rise from League One to the Premier League before playing an important role for The Reds last season as we returned to the top-flight, making 17 appearances in the process.

4 JOE WORRALL

DEFENDER DOB: 10/01/1997

Named permanent captain of Nottingham Forest in August 2022, Worrall has been with The Reds since joining the academy in 2011. Making his professional debut during a loan spell at Dagenham & Redbridge in January 2016, Worrall made his Forest debut the following season in October 2016. The defender has so far made over 190 appearances in the Garibaldi and captained The Reds in May's play-off final victory against Huddersfield Town at Wembley.

PREMIER LEAGUE 22/23
SQUAD

05 OREL MANGALA

MIDFIELDER DOB: 18/03/1998 COUNTRY: BELGIUM

Born in Belgium, the powerful midfielder started his career with Anderlecht before moving to German side VfB Stuttgart in 2017. After establishing himself in the Bundesliga, Mangala was called into the Belgium senior squad for the first time in March 2021 before joining The Reds in July. The midfielder made his Premier League debut away at Newcastle before making his first start in our home victory against West Ham United.

06 LOÏC MBE SOH

DEFENDER DOB: 13/06/2001 COUNTRY: CAMEROON

Born in Cameroon, Mbe Soh joined The Reds in September 2020 from French giants Paris Saint-Germain. The defender has represented France at youth level and made his Forest debut in September 2020, with his first goal coming in January 2021 against Middlesbrough.

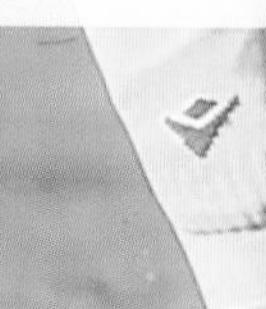

7 NECO WILLIAMS

DEFENDER DOB: 13/04/2001 COUNTRY: WALES

A summer signing from Liverpool, Williams appeared in the Premier League and the Champions League during his time with the Merseyside club and made his international debut for Wales in September 2020. Part of the side that won the Championship while on loan at Fulham last season, Williams made his Forest debut on the opening day of the 2022/23 campaign against Newcastle United.

08 JACK COLBACK

MIDFIELDER DOB: 24/10/1989 COUNTRY: ENGLAND

Born in Newcastle upon Tyne, Colback started his career with Sunderland before signing his first professional contract in 2008. The midfielder joined The Reds initially on loan in 2018 before making the move permanent in August 2020. Colback played a key role as Forest secured promotion to The Premier League last season, with his sensational volley against West Bromwich Albion securing the club's Goal of the Season award.

09 TAIWO AWONIYI

FORWARD DOB: 12/08/1997 COUNTRY: NIGERIA

Nigeria international forward Taiwo Awoniyi arrived on Trentside in June 2022 from Bundesliga side Union Berlin. The forward began his professional career with Liverpool in 2015 before enjoying loan spells in Germany, Holland and Belgium. Awoniyi scored his first goal for The Reds in a 1-0 win against West Ham United as Premier League football returned to The City Ground in August.

10 MORGAN GIBBS-WHITE

MIDFIELDER DOB: 27/01/2000 COUNTRY: ENGLAND

Morgan Gibbs-White arrived this summer after completing a transfer from Wolves. The England U21 international faced Forest in the Championship play-off semi-final last season, scoring at The City Ground before The Reds won on penalties. The attacking midfielder has linked up with Head Coach Steve Cooper in the past, playing under him during a loan spell with Swansea City and played a key role as the pair lifted the U17 World Cup trophy in 2017.

PREMIER LEAGUE 22/23
SQUAD

11 JESSE LINGARD

MIDFIELDER DOB: 15/12/1992 COUNTRY: ENGLAND

Born in Warrington, Lingard joined the Manchester United academy in 2000 and remained with The Red Devils until the summer of 2022 before joining Forest in July. The England international helped United win the FA Cup, League Cup and Europa League as well as featuring for the Three Lions at the 2018 FIFA World Cup.

12 JORDAN SMITH

GOALKEEPER DOB: 08/12/1994

A product of the Nottingham Forest academy, Smith joined The Reds at the age of seven and progressed through the ranks before signing his first professional contract in 2013. Making his Forest first-team debut in February 2017 against Norwich City, Smith's first clean sheet came a week later against Wigan Athletic. The goalkeeper has currently made over 45 appearances for The Reds.

PREMIER LEAGUE 22/23
SQUAD

13 WAYNE HENNESSEY

GOALKEEPER DOB: 24/01/1987

Capped over 100 times for Wales, Hennessey currently holds the record for the most clean sheets kept for his nation. The shot-stopper joined The Reds in July 2022 from Burnley and has over 180 Premier League appearances to his name following spells with Wolves and Crystal Palace and played an instrumental role as Wales secured World Cup qualification for the first time since 1958.

14 LEWIS O'BRIEN

MIDFIELDER DOB: 14/10/1998 COUNTRY: ENGLAND

Arriving in the summer from Huddersfield Town, O'Brien has quickly settled into life on Trentside. After a string of impressive performances, the energetic midfielder helped The Terriers reach the Championship play-off final last season before joining The Reds in July. Born in Colchester, O'Brien spent a season on loan with Bradford City in League One during the 2018/19 campaign.

15 HARRY TOFFOLO

DEFENDER DOB: 19/08/1995

After starting his career at Norwich City, Toffolo joined Huddersfield Town in January 2020 and was a key part of the Huddersfield Town team to reach the Championship play-off final against The Reds last season. The left-back's performances subsequently earned him a move to The City Ground in July before making his Premier League debut away at Newcastle United in August.

16 SAM SURRIDGE

FORWARD DOB: 28/07/1998 COUNTRY: ENGLAND

After signing for The Reds in January 2022, Surridge played a key role in helping Forest return to the Premier League after netting seven goals in 17 Championship appearances as well as scoring against Huddersfield Town in the Emirates FA Cup fifth round victory at The City Ground. The forward began his career with AFC Bournemouth before signing for Stoke City in August 2021.

PREMIER LEAGUE 22/23

SQUAD

17 ALEX MIGHTEN

FORWARD DOB: 11/04/2002 COUNTRY: USA

Another product of the Forest academy, Mighten joined The Reds in 2009 and made his debut against Arsenal in September 2019. The winger's first goal for the club came against Millwall in a Championship clash at The Den in December 2020. Mighten will spend the remainder of the 2022/23 campaign on loan at League One side Sheffield Wednesday.

19 MOUSSA NIAKHATÉ

DEFENDER DOB: 08/03/1996 COUNTRY: FRANCE

A summer signing from Bundesliga side Mainz 05, the defender has also previously featured for French sides FC Metz and Valenciennes. Arriving on Trentside in July, Niakhaté's Forest debut came on the opening day of the Premier League campaign away against Newcastle United. The 6′ 3″ centre back has also featured at youth level for France.

20 BRENNAN JOHNSON

FORWARD DOB: 23/05/2001 COUNTRY: ENGLAND

Born in Nottingham, Johnson joined the Forest academy in 2009 before making his senior debut against West Bromwich Albion in August 2019. The Wales international scored his first senior goal for The Reds in an East Midlands derby fixture against Derby County at Pride Park in August 2021. Johnson found the net on 19 occasions last season before scoring his first Premier League goal against Everton at Goodison Park in August.

21 CHEIKHOU KOUYATÉ

MIDFIELDER DOB: 21/12/1989 COUNTRY: SENEGAL

Born in Senegal, Kouyaté moved to Europe in 2006 before securing a move to the Premier League with West Ham in 2014 following six years with Anderlecht. The versatile midfielder can also play in defence and has a wealth of top-flight experience. Following four years with The Hammers, Kouyaté joined Crystal Palace in 2018 before signing for The Reds in August. Captain of the Senegal national team, Kouyaté helped his country lift the Africa Cup of Nations trophy in 2021.

PREMIER LEAGUE 22/23 SQUAD

22 RYAN YATES

MIDFIELDER DOB: 21/11/1997 COUNTRY: ENGLAND

Vice-captain Yates joined the Forest academy in 2005 before penning his first professional contract on Trentside in 2016. Loan spells followed including with Notts County and Scunthorpe United before establishing himself in The Reds' first team. A key member of the promotion winning squad, Yates netted eight goals from midfield as Forest returned to the Premier League.

23 REMO FREULER

MIDFIELDER DOB: 15/04/1992 COUNTRY: SWITZERLAND

Switzerland international captain Remo Freuler started his career with Winterthur before spells at Grasshoppers and Luzern lead to a Serie A move in 2016 to Atalanta. Spending six years in Italy, Freuler experienced captaining his side in the Champions League and also featured for his country at EURO 2020. The midfielder arrived on Trentside in August.

24 SERGE AURIER

DEFENDER DOB: 24/12/1992 COUNTRY: IVORY COAST

Former Paris Saint-Germain and Tottenham Hotspur full-back Serge Aurier arrived on Trentside in September following a season in Spain with Villareal. The Ivory Coast captain began his career with French side Lens and was part of the PSG side to win back-to-back league titles. Aurier helped his nation to win the Africa Cup of Nations in 2015 and was subsequently named in the team of the tournament.

25 EMMANUEL DENNIS

FORWARD DOB: 15/11/1997 COUNTRY: NIGERIA

Emmanuel Dennis moved to Europe in 2016 to join Ukrainian side Zorya Luhansk before moving to Belgium a year later to sign for Club Brugge. A Nigeria international, Dennis arrived in the Premier League at the beginning of the 2021/22 campaign and netted 10 goals for Watford. The forward signed for The Reds in August and made his City Ground debut against Tottenham Hotspur.

26 SCOTT McKENNA

DEFENDER DOB: 12/11/1996 COUNTRY: SCOTLAND

Born in Kirriemuir, the Scotland international defender joined The Reds from Aberdeen in September 2020 and has been a mainstay in our backline ever since. Part of the promotion-winning defence, McKenna was subsequently named Forest's 2021/22 Player of the Season after a campaign of strong performances to help seal The Reds' return to the Premier League.

PREMIER LEAGUE 22/23
SQUAD

27 OMAR RICHARDS

DEFENDER DOB: 15/02/1998 COUNTRY: ENGLAND

Born in Lewisham, left-back Richards signed for The Reds from German giants Bayern Munich in July. Following his professional debut for Reading in 2017, Richards would go on to make over 100 appearances for The Royals before securing a move to the Allianz Arena in May 2021. Richards featured 17 times last season as Bayern won the DFL-Supercup and Bundesliga title.

28 LOÏC BADÉ

DEFENDER DOB: 11/04/2000 COUNTRY: FRANCE

Badé joined The Reds on the final day of the 2022 summer transfer window on an initial loan deal from French Ligue 1 side Rennes. Capped at France U21 level, the 6ft 3″ defender began his career with Le Havre before moving to Lens in 2020. Joining Rennes the following season, Badé has experience in the UEFA Europa League and scored his first professional goal in the competition in November 2021.

30 WILLY BOLY

DEFENDER DOB: 03/02/1991 COUNTRY: FRANCE

Defender Willy Boly signed for The Reds in September from Wolverhampton Wanderers. The Ivory Coast international moved to England from Porto to join the Molineux side in 2017, helping them win promotion to the Premier League in his first campaign. Boly has also previously featured for Braga and Auxerre and made his international debut in November 2020.

32 RENAN LODI

DEFENDER DOB: 08/04/1998 COUNTRY: BRAZIL

Brazil international defender Renan Lodi arrived on Trentside from Spanish giants Atlético Madrid in August, initially on loan for the 2022/23 season. After making his debut for Brazil in 2019, Lodi was a key component in the Atlético side that were crowned La Liga champions in 2020. Prior to his spell in Spain, Lodi rose through the ranks at Athletico Paranaense and helped the Brazilian side lift the Copa Sudamericana and Campeonato Paranaense in 2018.

MULTIPLE CHOICE

Here are ten Multiple Choice questions to challenge your footy knowledge!

Good luck...

ANSWERS ON PAGE 62

1. What was the name of Tottenham Hotspur's former ground?

A) White Rose Park
B) White Foot Way
C) White Hart Lane

2. Which club did Steven Gerrard leave to become Aston Villa manager?

A) Liverpool,
B) Glasgow Rangers
C) LA Galaxy

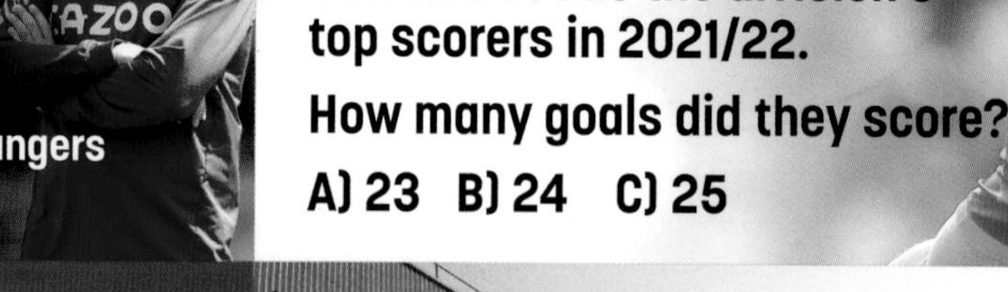

3. Mohamed Salah and Son Heung-min were joint winners of the Premier League Golden Boot as the division's top scorers in 2021/22.

How many goals did they score?

A) 23 B) 24 C) 25

4. What is the nationality of Manchester United boss Erik ten Hag?

A) Swiss B) Dutch
C) Swedish

5. Where do Everton play their home games?

A) Goodison Road
B) Goodison Way
C) Goodison Park

6. From which club did Arsenal sign goalkeeper Aaron Ramsdale?

A) Sheffield United
B) Stoke City
C) AFC Bournemouth

7. What is Raheem Sterling's middle name?

A) Shaun
B) Shaquille
C) Silver

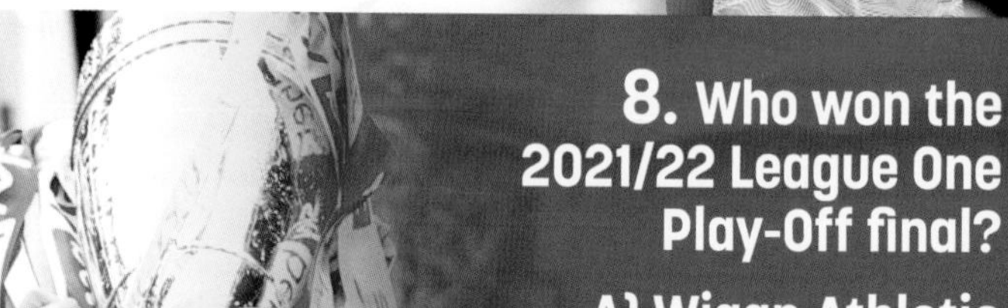

8. Who won the 2021/22 League One Play-Off final?

A) Wigan Athletic
B) Sunderland
C) Rotherham United

9. How many times have Forest won the European Cup?

A) Once
B) Twice
C) Three times

10. Which League One club was Brennan Johnson loaned to in 2020/21?

A) Crewe Alexandra
B) Ipswich Town
C) Lincoln City

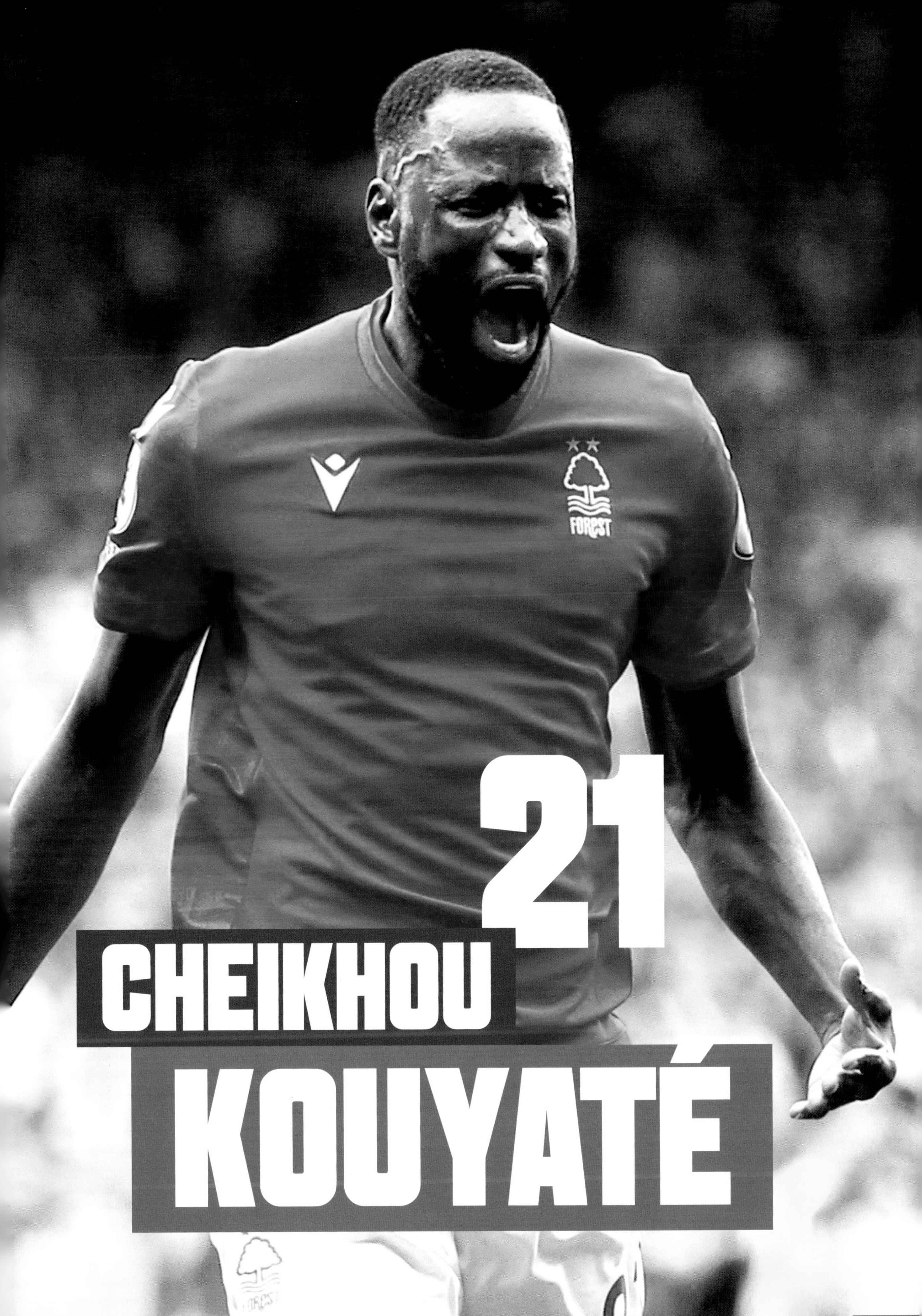
21
CHEIKHOU
KOUYATÉ
FOREST

YOU ARE PREMIER

CLASSIC FAN'TASTIC

Robin Hood is hiding in the crowd in five different places as Forest fans celebrate promotion to the Premier League in 2021/22. **Can you find all five?**

ANSWERS ON PAGE 62

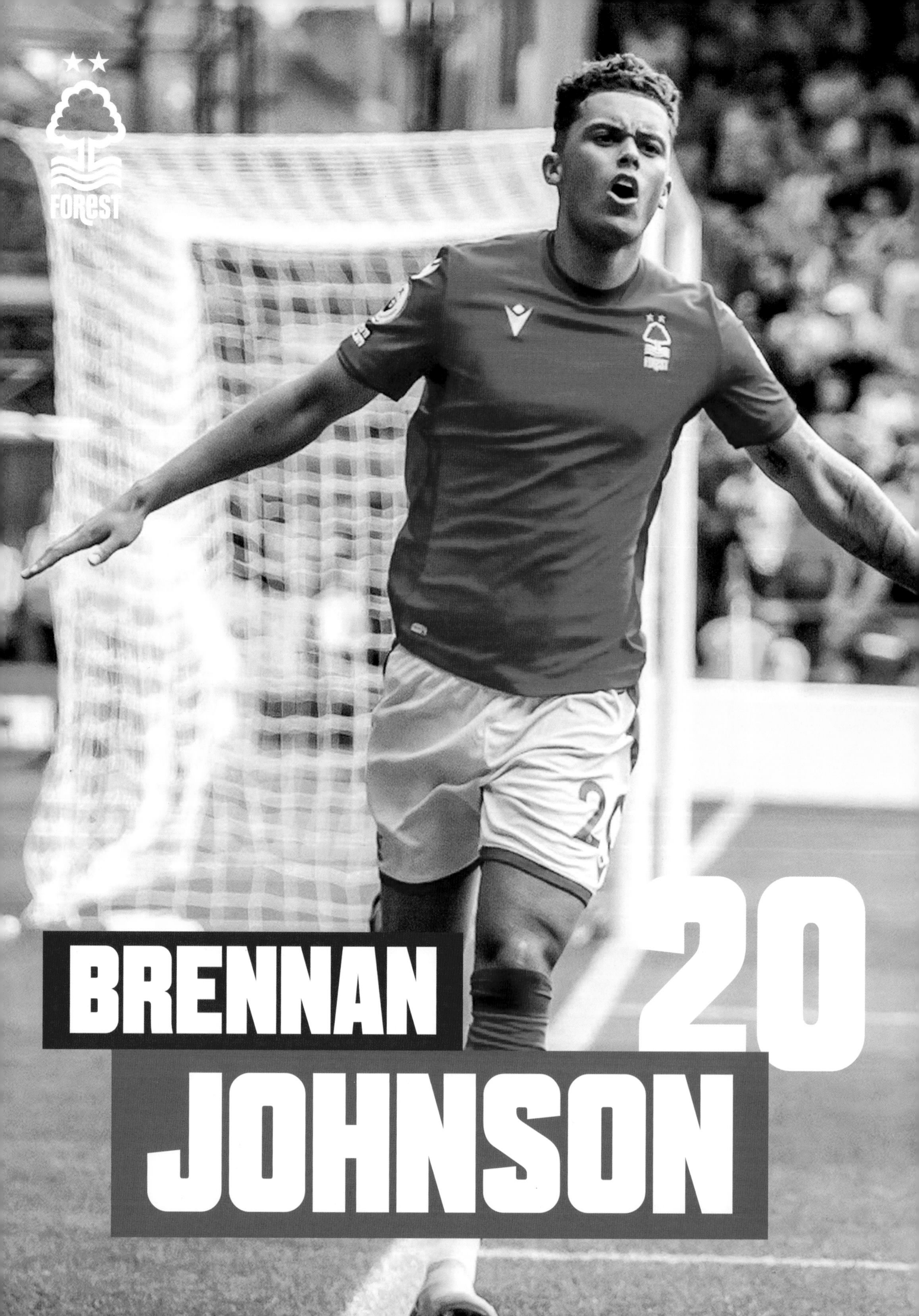

BRENNAN JOHNSON 20

ANSWERS ON PAGE 62

Close control in tight situations creates havoc in opposition defences - particularly when receiving the ball in the air - and nine times out of ten, when a striker receives the ball, he has his back to goal.

SOCCER SKILLS

RECEIVING THE BALL

Quite often the ball will arrive in the air, and good strikers have to be able to cope with that - controlling and turning in one movement, ready for the instant shot.

EXERCISE 1

In an area 20m x 10m, two players A and A2 test the man in the middle, B, by initially throwing the ball at him in the air, with the instruction to turn and play in to the end man - if possible using only two touches.

The middle player is changed regularly, and to make things more realistic, the end players progress to chipping the ball into the middle.

The middle player is asked to receive and turn using chest, thigh, or instep.

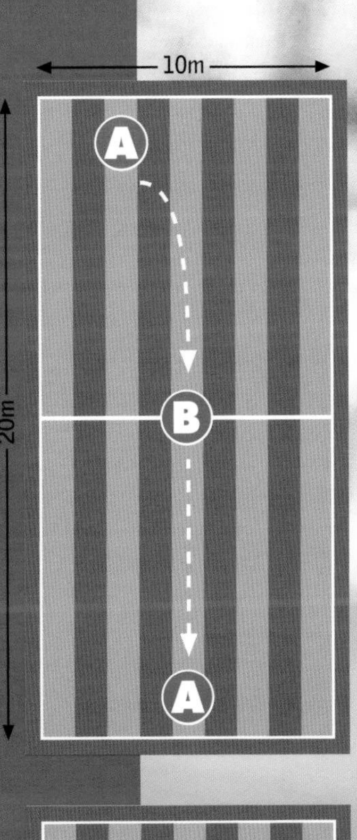

KEY FACTORS

1. Assess flight early - get in position.
2. Cushion the ball.
3. Be half-turned as you receive.

EXERCISE 2

A progression of this exercise is the following, where the ball is chipped or driven in to the striker from varying positions. He has to receive with his back to goal, and using just two touches in total if possible, shoot past the keeper into the goal!

To make this even more difficult, a defender can be brought in eventually. For younger children, the 'servers' should throw the ball to ensure consistent quality.

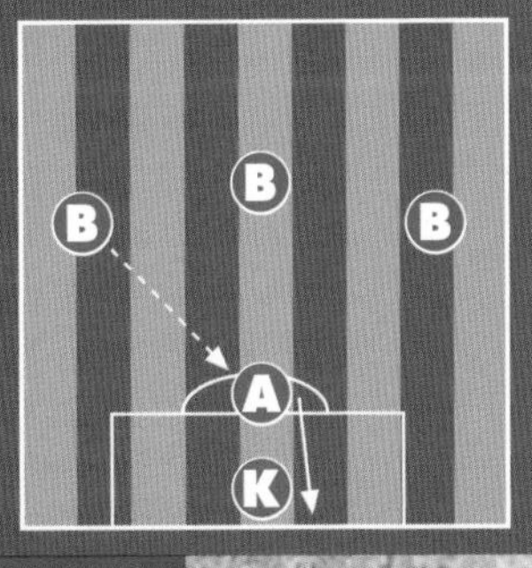

FOREST

TRAIN TO WIN

Making sure that you are fit, healthy and fully prepared is key to success in whatever challenge you are taking on. Those three factors are certainly vital for professional footballers and also for any young aspiring player who plays for his or her school or local football team. The importance of fitness, health and preparation are key factors behind the work that goes into preparing the Nottingham Forest players to perform at their maximum on matchday.

The Forest players will need to demonstrate peak levels of fitness if they want to feature in Steve Cooper's team. Before anyone can think of pulling on a smart red shirt and stepping out at the City Ground, they will have had to perform well at the Training Ground to have shown the manager, his coaches and fitness staff that they are fully fit and ready for the physical challenges that await them on a matchday.

Regardless of whether training takes place at the training ground or at the stadium, the players' fitness remains an all-important factor. Of course time spent practicing training drills and playing small-sided games will help a player's fitness but there is lots of work undertaken just to ensure maximum levels of fitness are reached.

Away from the training pitches the players will spend a great deal of time in the gymnasium partaking in their own personal work-outs. Bikes, treadmills and weights will all form part of helping the players reach and maintain a top level of fitness.

Over the course of a week the players will take part in many warm-up and aerobic sessions and even complete yoga and pilates classes to help with core strength and general fitness. The strength and conditioning coaches at the club work tirelessly to do all they can to make sure that the players you see in action are at their physical peak come kick-off.

While the manager and his staff will select the team and agree the tactics, analysts will provide the players and staff with details on the opposition's strengths, weaknesses and their likely approach to the match.

Suffice to say the training ground is a busy place and no stone is left unturned in preparation for the big match!

PLAYER OF THE YEAR

Despite conceding 12 goals in our opening seven games of the season, Forest went on to boast the second-best defensive record in the Championship in 2021/22. The Reds shipped only 40 goals in 46 league matches last season - only Champions Fulham conceded fewer goals, conceding 39 times.

The addition of Steve Cook in January certainly helped to solidify the defensive line even further, slotting into the centre of defence in-between Joe Worrall and Scott McKenna. Into his second season on Trentside, McKenna established himself as an important player as The Reds secured a long-awaited return to the Premier League.

The Scotland international scored in our first league game back at The City Ground, rising highest to head home from Philip Zinckernagel's free kick. As alluded to previously, the arrival of Steve Cooper prompted a change to a back three, seeing McKenna slot in as a left-sided centre-half and providing balance in defence.

McKenna's driving runs forward were regular features as the season went on. Our fourth and final goal in the resounding victory at Blackpool typified the freedom given to the Scotsman due to a change in system, as he intercepted a loose pass, drove forward and put the ball on a plate for Sam Surridge to fire into the net.

McKenna's lung-busting run in our home fixture against Bristol City in February was also mightily impressive – the defender receiving the ball in his own half, motoring forward, exchanging passes with Max Lowe on the byline before James Garner calmly found the bottom corner for 2-0.

Not just offensively and defensively, but off the pitch too, McKenna made his mark, named our PFA Community Champion for 2021/22.

BOXT

?????
BOXT
BOXT

BOXT

DREAM TEAM

Pick your ultimate Nottingham Forest dream team and design them a kit!

CLUB SEARCH

EVERY TEAM IN THE PREMIER LEAGUE IS HIDDEN IN THE GRID, EXCEPT FOR ONE... CAN YOU WORK OUT WHICH ONE?

M A S D D E T I N U R E T S E H C N A M
K P W H M F Y A G I S G F Z E N O P H S
S M A N C H E S T E R C I T Y J B F O E
W N A E L T G I R C I A S B D R I U J T
K E F R U P S T O H M A H N E T T O T G
H Q S B D D B L B S V U S N D H O R S B
C A F T X E H O R Y S N T H A K J M E E
A G Y J H W T U O Q C F N M C A L V R C
U O U T S A R I L P O D P K L P E A O A
H T S U I G M A N R A T P L U R T D F L
T P T H P C N U D U O M I S T A F E M A
U I T W V E R A N N E V F O W E P G A P
O R M E S J W E P I N L N L E S U L H L
M O K R O S U V T O T A T M N L C I G A
E M A H L U F G T S K E K S D E B M N T
N N L D Q F C S N P E W D H A H O A I S
R S I A J B A O A S Y C B O O C N X T Y
U H D R Z L O O P R E V I L U L W J T R
O T E C D E T I N U S D E E L R A E O C
B R I G H T O N & H O V E A L B I O N T

Arsenal
Aston Villa
Bournemouth
Brentford
Brighton & Hove Albion

Chelsea
Crystal Palace
Everton
Fulham
Leeds United

Leicester City
Liverpool
Manchester City
Manchester United
Newcastle United

Nottingham Forest
Southampton
Tottenham Hotspur
West Ham United
Wolverhampton Wanderers

ANSWERS ON PAGE 62

PREMIER LEAGUE DANGER MEN

20 TOP-FLIGHT STARS TO WATCH OUT FOR DURING 2022/23...

ARSENAL

GABRIEL JESUS

The Gunners completed the signing of Brazilian international striker Gabriel Jesus from Premier League champions Manchester City in July 2022.

A real penalty-box predator, Jesus netted 95 goals in 236 appearances in a trophy-laden spell for City and Arsenal will be hopeful he can continue his impressive goals-to-games ratio at the Emirates Stadium.

ASTON VILLA

EMI BUENDIA

Now in his second season at Villa Park, following a big money move from Norwich City, a great deal will be expected of Argentinean international midfielder Emi Buendia in 2022/23.

A highly skilful and creative player, Buendia has the ability to create chances for teammates and score vital goals himself.

BOURNEMOUTH

KIEFFER MOORE

Giant front-man Kieffer Moore chipped in with four goals in three games to help Bournemouth secure promotion to the Premier League last season.

The former Cardiff City man will be keen to prove his worth at Premier League level in 2022/23 in order to cement his place in Wales' squad for the 2022 FIFA World Cup finals in Qatar.

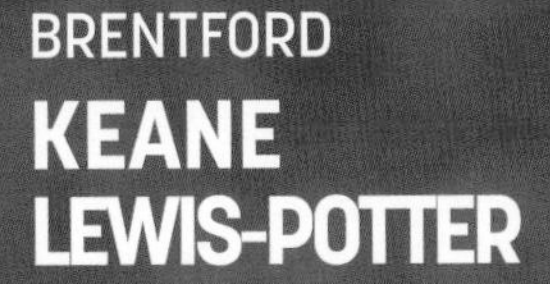

BRENTFORD

KEANE LEWIS-POTTER

England U21 star Keane Lewis-Potter enjoyed an exceptional Championship campaign with Hull City in 2021/22 and that prompted Brentford to spend a club record fee to bring the exciting 21-year-old to West London.

A true attacker who can operate off of either flank, Lewis-Potter will be relishing the challenge of showcasing his skills at Premier League level.

BRIGHTON & HA

LEANDRO TROSSARD

After weighing in with eight Premier League goals last season, Belgian international winger Trossard has widely become recognised as the Seagulls' main creative force.

Hugging the left touchline and cutting inside to play in a teammate or striking for goal himself, Trossard is another player who will be looking to feature in the forthcoming World Cup.

CRYSTAL PALACE

WILFRIED ZAHA

Players may come and go at Selhurst Park, but the constant threat offered by the Crystal Palace club legend Wilfried Zaha remains firmly in place.

An exciting forward who loves to take opponents on in one-on-one situations, Zaha has now amassed over 400 appearances for the club across his two spells at Selhurst Park, and will be looking to fly the Eagles into the top half of the Premier League table.

CHELSEA

MASON MOUNT

Having progressed through the academy system at Stamford Bridge, attacking midfielder Mason Mount has become one of the first names on both the Chelsea and England teamsheet.

Mount hit eleven Premier League goals last season and head coach Graham Potter will be keen to see more of the same as Chelsea look to put pressure on Liverpool and Manchester City in 2022/23.

EVERTON

JORDAN PICKFORD

Firmly established as first choice keeper for club and country, Jordan has been a reliable last line of defence for the Toffees since joining the club in summer 2017.

A host of match-saving games last season were rewarded with the Player of the Season award and the England No.1 has now played over 200 games for Everton.

FULHAM

ALEKSANDAR MITROVIC

Having fired home a record-breaking 43 Championship goals for Fulham in their title-winning campaign last season, all eyes will be on Aleksandar Mitrovic in 2022/23.

If Fulham are to shake off their yo-yo club tag, then the top-flight goalscoring form of their powerful Serbian striker is going to be key.

LIVERPOOL

MOHAMED SALAH

Together with goalkeeper Alisson and inspirational defender Virgil van Dijk, Liverpool forward Mo Salah has been the catalyst for the Reds' success in recent seasons.

The Egyptian superstar jointly topped the Premier League scoring charts with Spurs' Son Heung-min last season as Liverpool enjoyed a domestic cup double.

LEEDS UNITED

PATRICK BAMFORD

After suffering an injury-hit 2021/22, Leeds United striker Patrick Bamford will be hopeful that 2022/23 offers him the chance to demonstrate the form that won him a first full England cap in September 2021.

A versatile front man who can play as a lone striker or in a pair, Bamford can also operate as an attacking midfielder from either flank.

LEICESTER CITY

JAMIE VARDY

The goalscoring hero of Leicester City's sensational 2014/15 Premier League title triumph, striker Jamie Vardy once again topped the Foxes' scoring charts last season.

An energetic forward, full of running, Jamie never gives defenders a moment of peace, and will once again be the one to watch for goals at King Power Stadium in 2022/23.

MANCHESTER CITY

ERLING HAALAND

Manchester City pulled off the biggest summer transfer coup when they lured Norwegian striker Erling Haaland from Borussia Dortmund to the Etihad Stadium for 2022/23.

Boasting a phenomenal strike rate at Dortmund and with his national team too, Haaland is sure to bring goals galore to the Premier League champions.

MANCHESTER UNITED

BRUNO FERNANDES

Attacking midfielder Bruno has become the heartbeat of the Red Devils' forward play since signing from Sporting Lisbon.

Blessed with a wide range of passing skills, the 28-year-old Portuguese international has the knack of unlocking even the tightest of defences.

TOTTENHAM HOTSPUR

SON HEUNG-MIN

South Korean superstar Son ended the 2021/22 season by picking up the Premier League Golden Boot as joint top goalscorer along with Liverpool's Mohamed Salah.

Forming an almost telepathic partnership with England captain Harry Kane, Tottenham Hotspur will certainly be a team to watch if Son repeats his lethal form in front of goal again in 2022/23.

NEWCASTLE UNITED

BRUNO GUIMARAES

After joining the Magpies from Lyon in January 2022, Brazilian midfielder Bruno has become a real cult hero with the fans at St James' Park.

Bruno scored five Premier League goals in 17 games last season and looks set to be one of the first names on Eddie Howe's teamsheet in 22/23.

WEST HAM UNITED

JARROD BOWEN

Blessed with the ability to operate in a variety of attacking positions, Jarrod Bowen enjoyed an exceptional 2021/22 campaign.

The 25-year-old netted 18 goals in all competitions and made 51 appearances as the Hammers enjoyed a top-half finish and reached the semi-finals of the Europa League. He was also handed an England debut in June 2022.

NOTTINGHAM FOREST

DEAN HENDERSON

Forest made a real statement of intent following their promotion to the Premier League when they completed the season-long loan signing of the Man United keeper.

Capped by England, Dean will hope his City Ground performances can push him into England boss Gareth Southgate's thoughts for the 2022 FIFA World Cup finals in Qatar.

SOUTHAMPTON

JAMES WARD-PROWSE

One of the very best dead ball deliverers, Saints skipper Ward-Prowse has progressed through the academy ranks at St Mary's to play over 350 first-team games for the club.

James is another England star who will hope to be on the plane for Qatar 2022.

WOLVES

GONCALO GUEDES

Wanderers boosted their attacking options when they completed the signing of Portugal forward Goncalo Guedes from Valencia at the start of the 2022/23 season.

Capped on over 30 occasions by Portugal, the 25-year-old is well known to Wolves' boss Bruno Lage having played for him at Benfica earlier in his career.

FOREST
TAIWO
AWONIYI
9

TRUE OR FALSE?

Here are ten fun footy True or False teasers for you to tackle!

Good luck...

ANSWERS ON PAGE 62

1. England star Harry Kane has only ever played club football for Spurs

2. The FIFA World Cup in 2026 is due to be hosted in the USA, Mexico and Canada

3. Manchester City's former ground was called Maine Park

4. Liverpool's Jurgen Klopp has never managed the German national team

5. Gareth Southgate succeeded Roy Hodgson as England manager

6. Manchester United's Old Trafford has the largest capacity in the Premier League

7. Jordan Pickford began his career at Everton

8. Huddersfield Town's nickname is the Terriers

9. Forest left-back Harry Toffolo began his career with Norwich City

10. Brennan Johnson made his Wales debut against Finland

BOXT
32Red

2021/22 SEASON REVIEW

The 2021/22 campaign. A truly memorable season for all Nottingham Forest supporters as The Reds returned to the Premier League after 23 years.

But it wasn't always straight-forward.

The Reds began the season terribly, with six defeats and zero wins from the first seven games signalling the club's worst start to a campaign for 108 years.

A 2-0 home defeat to Middlesbrough was the final straw for Chris Hughton, but a 2-0 away win over Huddersfield Town under interim boss Steven Reid in September was the start of a new era.

On the 21st of September, Steve Cooper was appointed the new Head Coach of Nottingham Forest, with the Welshman arriving at The City Ground after recording back-to-back top-six finishes during a two-year stint at Swansea City.

Cooper hit the ground running upon his arrival on Trentside. Forest won four of his five games at the helm and lost only one game between September and Boxing Day as The Reds motored their way up the Championship.

The turn of the year saw the FA Cup campaign get underway, with The Reds coinciding their impressive league form with an even more impressive cup run, defeating Premier League sides Arsenal and Leicester City before narrowly losing 1-0 to Liverpool in the quarter finals.

In the Championship, though, things were going very smoothly indeed. The Reds picked up 14 wins from 19 matches ahead of a trip to AFC Bournemouth in May, with Cooper's men sat within three points of the Cherries heading into the final two games of the campaign.

Forest were unable to pip Scott Parker's side in the race for automatic promotion, losing by a goal to nil at the Vitality Stadium and leaving the play-offs as the only remaining route to the Premier League.

Finishing in fourth place on 80 points, the club's highest league finish since 2010 and highest points tally at the level since 1998, Forest were drawn against Sheffield United over two semi-final legs.

Goals from Jack Colback and Brennan Johnson secured a 2-1 first leg win at Bramall Lane, but despite Johnson putting The Reds 3-1 up on aggregate early in the second leg, United fought back, levelling the scores to 3-3 on aggregate and sending the tie to a penalty shootout, with Brice Samba saving three penalty kicks to send Forest to Wembley.

So this was it. Forest against Huddersfield Town, at Wembley, with Premier League football at stake.

In what was a tense affair under the arch, The Reds edged it. James Garner's first half strike, which found the top corner via a Levi Colwill deflection, was enough to end a 23-year exile away from England's top flight, sparking jubilation in the red end at Wembley.

The following day, Nottingham came together to paint Market Square red, as the players and staff took to the Council House balcony to celebrate the achievement.

sky bet
BOXT
JOHNSON

EFL
sky bet
sky bet
EFL

sky bet

WHICH BALL?

Can you work out which is the actual match ball in these two action pics?

ANSWERS ON PAGE 62

NAME THE SEASON

Can you recall the campaign when these magic moments occurred?

Good luck...

ANSWERS ON PAGE 62

1. In which season did Chelsea last win the UEFA Champions League?

2. When were Manchester United last Premier League champions?

3. At the end of which season were England crowned World Cup winners?

4. In which season did Aleksandar Mitrovic net 43 Championship goals for Fulham?

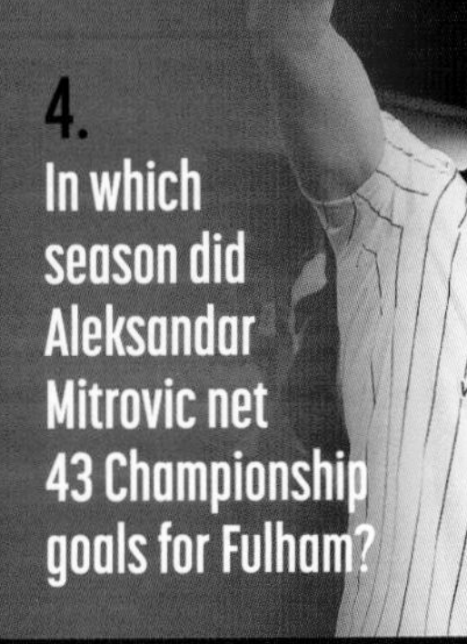

5. In which season did Leicester City become Premier League champions?

6. When did Tottenham Hotspur last reach the League Cup final?

7. In which season were Sheffield United last promoted to the Premier League?

8. When did Manchester City win their first Premier League title?

9. During which season did Jack Colback make his Forest debut?

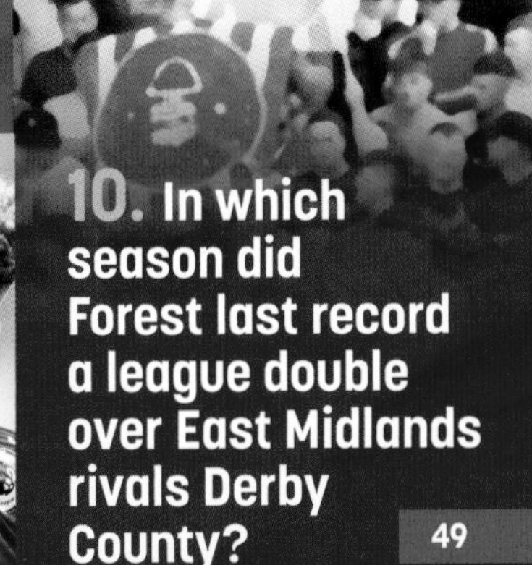

10. In which season did Forest last record a league double over East Midlands rivals Derby County?

DEAN HENDERSON

1

SPOT THE DIFFERENCE?

Can you spot the eight differences between these two photographs?

ANSWERS ON PAGE 62

ANSWERS ON PAGE 62

WHO ARE YER?

Can you figure out who each of these Forest stars is?

10 MORGAN GIBBS-WHITE

TRUE COLOURS

Can you colour in this picture of Morgan Gibbs-White?

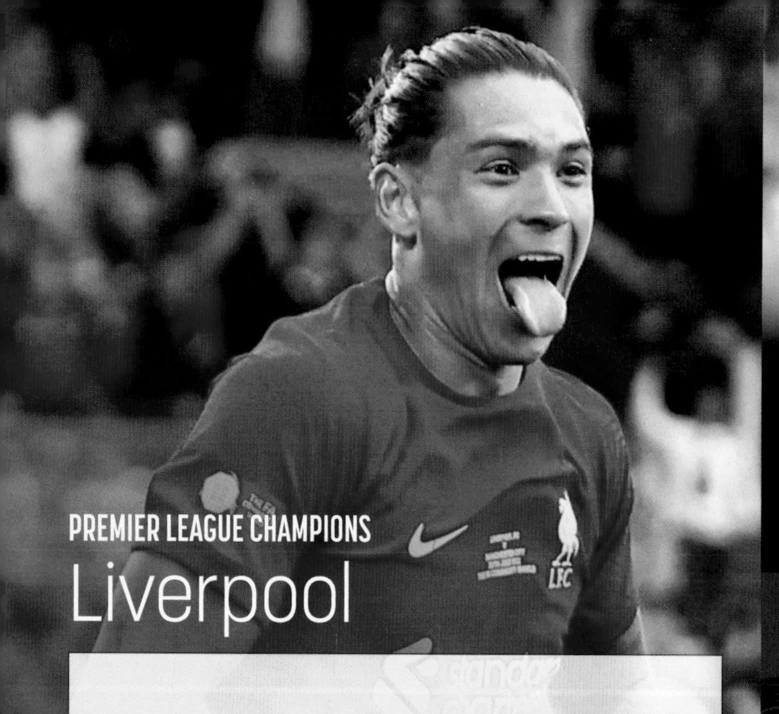

PREMIER LEAGUE CHAMPIONS

Liverpool

FAST FORWARD

Do your predictions for 2022/23 match our own?...

CHAMPIONSHIP WINNERS

Watford

CHAMPIONSHIP

CHAMPIONSHIP RUNNERS-UP

Norwich City

PREMIER LEAGUE

PREMIER LEAGUE RUNNERS-UP

Chelsea

PREMIER LEAGUE TOP SCORER

Erling Haaland

CHAMPIONSHIP TOP SCORER

Michael Obafemi

LEAGUE ONE TOP SCORER

Conor Chaplin

FA CUP

FA CUP WINNERS

Brighton & HA

LEAGUE CUP WINNERS

Nottingham Forest

LEAGUE CUP

LEAGUE ONE CHAMPIONS

Ipswich Town

CHAMPIONS LEAGUE

CHAMPIONS LEAGUE WINNERS

Real Madrid

LEAGUE ONE RUNNERS-UP

Oxford United

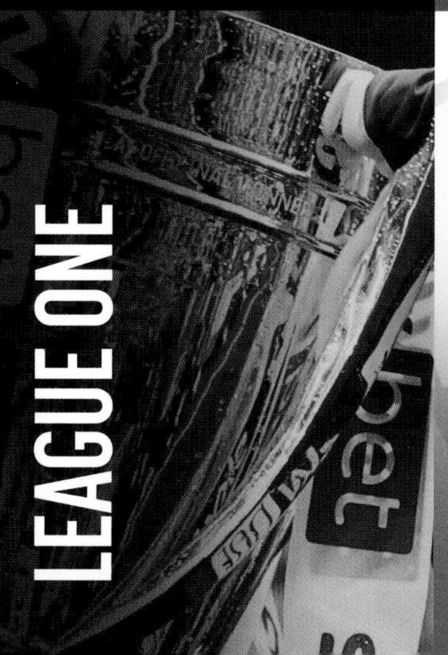

LEAGUE ONE

EUROPA LEAGUE WINNERS

Roma

EUROPA LEAGUE

NUMBER OF SEASONS WITH NOTTINGHAM FOREST:

7

NOTTINGHAM FOREST LEAGUE APPEARANCES:

206

NOTTINGHAM FOREST LEAGUE GOALS:

50

PLAYER OF THE SEASON WINNER:

1982/83

LEGEND

STEVE HODGE

NOTTINGHAM FOREST ACHIEVEMENTS:

Full Members Cup winners 1988/89
League Cup winners 1989/89 and 1989/90
FA Cup runners-up 1990/91

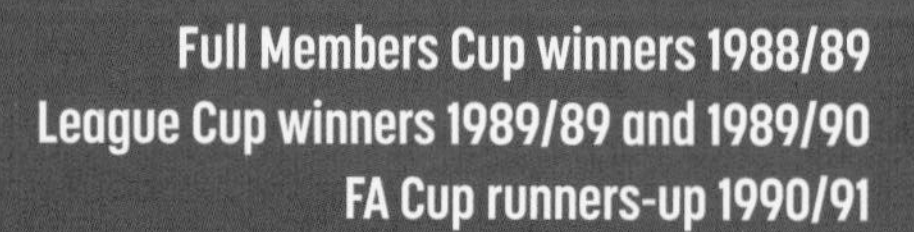

MAJOR STRENGTH:

A great ability to surge forward and score goals from midfield

INTERNATIONAL ACTION:

Steve won nine of his 24 England caps during his second spell at Forest

FINEST HOUR:

Hodge's run into the box won the penalty that set Forest on their way to League Cup glory at Wembley in 1989

Central midfield stars Steve Hodge and Roy Keane were two of the most impressive midfield players to pull on the famous Forest shirt and both made a big impression at the City Ground.

Hodge and Keane were clear match winners on their day and blessed with the skill and talent to turn games in Forest's favour. With the ability to score goals and create chances for teammates, these two former Forest stars were both real crowd favourites at the City Ground. Unsurprisingly they both also enjoyed great international careers too. But who was the best? That's for you to decide and here are a few facts and figures from their time in red and white to help you reach your conclusion...

It's a tough call...!

LEGEND

ROY KEANE

NUMBER OF SEASONS WITH NOTTINGHAM FOREST:

3

NOTTINGHAM FOREST LEAGUE APPEARANCES:

114

NOTTINGHAM FOREST LEAGUE GOALS:

22

PLAYER OF THE SEASON WINNER:

Never

NOTTINGHAM FOREST ACHIEVEMENTS:

FA Cup runners-up 1990/91, Full Members Cup winner 1991/92, League Cup runners-up 1991/92

MAJOR STRENGTH:

A real midfielder competitor, Keane led by example with his desire to win the ball and retain possession

INTERNATIONAL ACTION:

Roy made his international debut for the Republic of Ireland while at Forest and went on to play for his country on 67 occasions

FINEST HOUR:

En route to Wembley, it was Keane who struck the only goal of the game in Forest's FA Cup quarter-final victory over Norwich City in March 1991

IDENTIFY THE STAR

Can you put a name to the football stars in these ten teasers?

Good luck...

ANSWERS ON PAGE 62

1. Manchester City's title-winning 'keeper Ederson shared the 2021/22 Golden Glove award for the number of clean sheets with which Premier League rival?

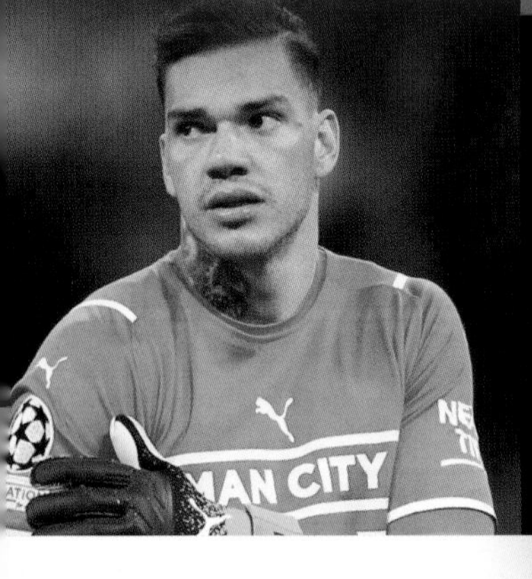

2. Which Portuguese superstar re-joined Manchester United in the 2021/22 season?

3. Can you name the Brazilian forward who joined Aston Villa in May 2022 following a loan spell at Villa Park?

4. Who became Arsenal manager in 2019?

5. Who scored the winning goal in the 2021/22 UEFA Champions League final?

6. After 550 games for the West Ham United, which long-serving midfielder announced his retirement in 2022?

7. Who took the mantle of scoring Brentford's first Premier League goal?

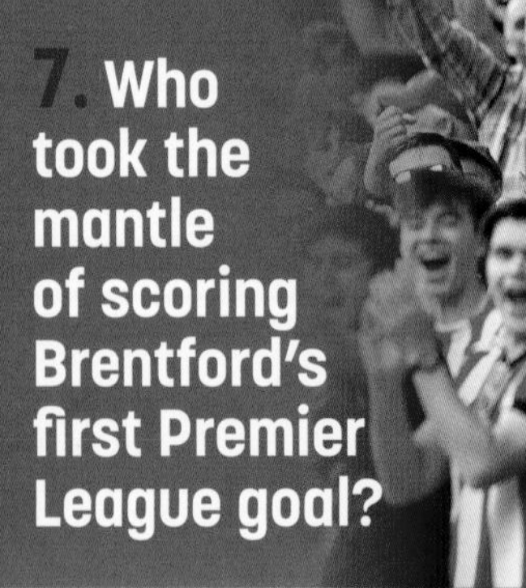

8. Who scored the final goal for Manchester City in their 2021/22 Premier League title-winning season?

9. Which Wales international joined Forest from Liverpool in July 2022?

10. Can you name the goalkeeper who joined Forest on loan ahead of the 2022/23 Premier League campaign?

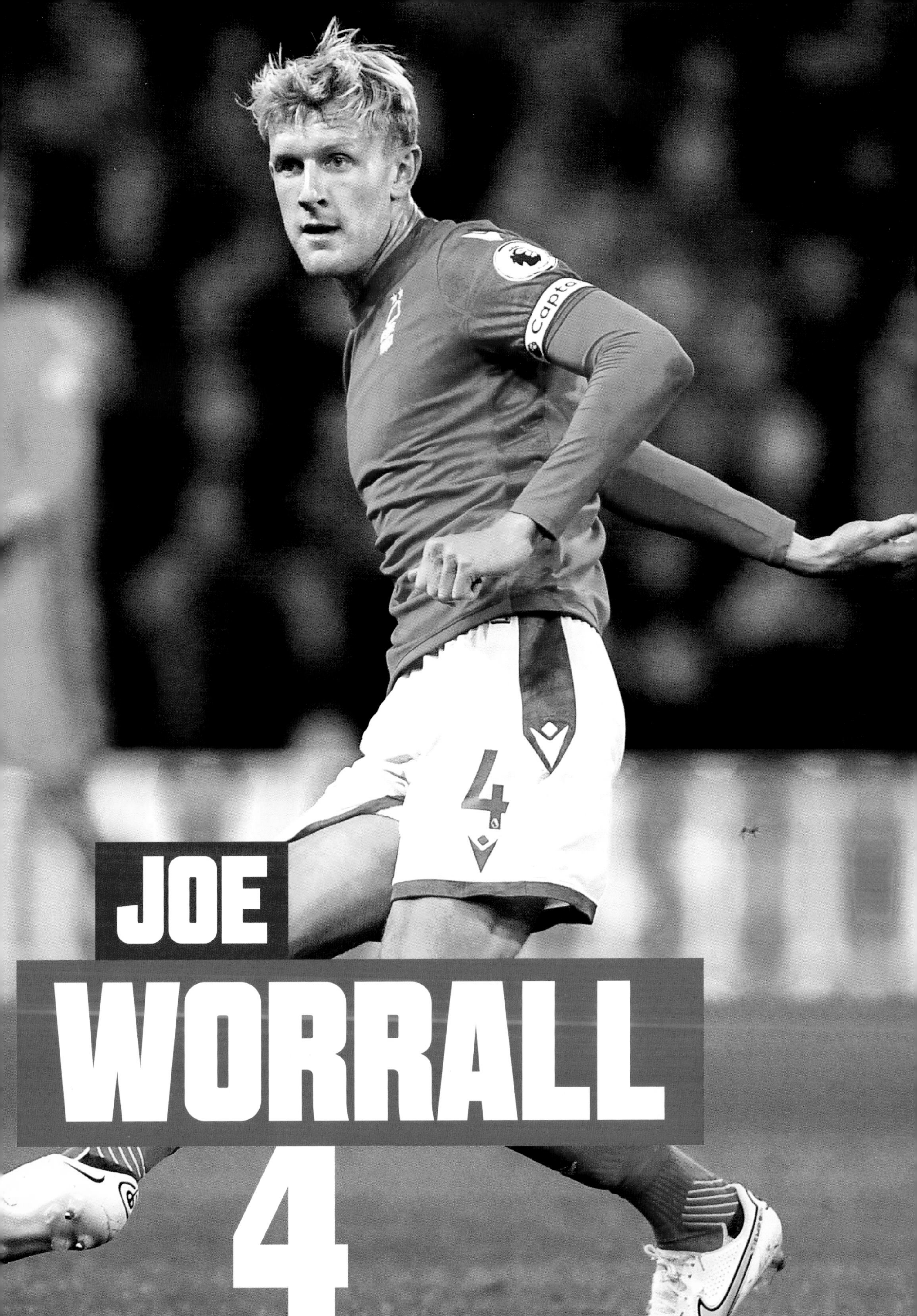
JOE
WORRALL
4

ANSWERS

PAGE 24 • MULTIPLE CHOICE

1. C. 2. B. 3. A. 4. B. 5. C. 6. A. 7. B. 8. B. 9. B. 10. C.

PAGE 26 • CLASSIC FAN'TASTIC

PAGE 35 • CLUB SEARCH

Wolverhampton Wanderers

PAGE 41 • TRUE OR FALSE?

1. False, Harry played on loan for Leyton Orient, Millwall, Norwich City & Leicester City. 2. True. 3. False, it was called Maine Road. 4. True. 5. False, Gareth succeeded Sam Allardyce. 6. True. 7. False, Jordan began his career at Sunderland. 8. True. 9. True. 10. False, he made his debut against USA.

PAGE 48 • WHICH BALL?

PAGE 49 • NAME THE SEASON

1. 2020/21. 2. 2012/13. 3. 1965/66. 4. 2021/22. 5. 2015/16. 6. 2020/21. 7. 2018/19. 8. 2011/12. 9. 2017/18. 10. 2010/11.

PAGE 51 • SPOT THE DIFFERENCE →

PAGE 52 • WHO ARE YER?

1. Scott McKenna. 2. Orel Mangala. 3. Jesse Lingard. 4. Brennan Johnson. 5. Jack Colback. 6. Remo Freuler. 7. Loic Mbe Soh. 8. Cheikhou Kouyaté.

PAGE 60 • IDENTIFY THE STAR

1. Allison Becker. 2. Cristiano Ronaldo. 3. Philippe Coutinho. 4. Mikel Arteta. 5. Vinicius Junior. 6. Mark Noble. 7. Sergi Canos. 8. Ilkay Gundogan. 9. Neco Williams. 10. Dean Henderson.